Starting Points
Poetic Invitations to Conversation

by

Anthony Kasozi

Grosvenor House Publishing Limited

This book is published by
Grosvenor House Publishing Ltd
Link House
140 The Broadway, Tolworth, Surrey, KT6 7HT.
www.grosvenorhousepublishing.co.uk

A CIP record for this book
is available from the British Library

Paperback ISBN 978-1-83615-272-9
Hardback ISBN 978-1-83615-271-2
eBook ISBN 978-1-83615-273-6

"*There is no perfect dialogue.
Only starting points.
Invitations to conversations.
That perchance, may with
time unfold into deeper
meaning... **understanding** ...
That reveals what this moment
hides and yet yearns to yield.
And now presents
here in exhibition.*"

Contents

Introduction

When I started writing the poems that make up this book, I didn't know what I was doing. I certainly did not appreciate the journey I was embarking on. Now, many years later, it feels clearer, yet still unfolding; and I feel lucky and pleased to be able to share this with you.

This book started as a scattering of poems, written when feeling provoked by instances that fell across my path. I didn't see myself as a poet, merely a scribbler, content to put my musings down on pieces of paper and in notebooks, to be revisited as and when time and occasion permitted.

Over the years, several poems emerged which stood on their own, until the summer of 2023, when on vacation on the Greek island of Antipaxos, I put them all together into a collection. Realizing for the first time, that this could be some kind of anthology.

Returning home to Surrey, this anthology took shape, the poems being honed and changed, and the odd new one being added, until one day, while in spiritual and life conversation with my supervisor, Lindsay Wittenberg, she commented that I was at my most "alive" when sitting with and contemplating questions. This led to another poem, "My Questions" - which I shared with Lindsay.

Back at work and talking with my colleague Anne-Marie Miller, a skilled illustrator with whom I had collaborated in the past, it occurred to me that what I wrote and what others gathered as insights from my writings could be of interest. *The idea of reading and listening to the poems and seeing Illustrations of the same poems could be a provocation and invitation into conversation.*

Anne-Marie agreed to illustrate the poems. She listened to me reading them and then drew what they evoked and provoked, in her. We began with her listening to Lindsay and me discussing "My Questions", then she moved on to illustrate the others, drawing in response to how each one touched her. In time the poems came together into chapters, which fell into themes that ran and run through my life:

Mirror... Stewardship... Still-Life... Calling... Mystery.

And then a title came:

Starting Points - Invitations to Conversation

What happened next was unexpected, not part of the plan. From out of a cloudless sky I was diagnosed with oesophageal cancer of the upper gastrointestinal tract.

So began a difficult, darker part of the journey. The first step into the shadowlands was settling on a diagnosis, being part of conversations I'd never had before, with people I'd never met, looking to answer the question: how far had the cancer spread?

The second step was working through what treatment was possible and what could be offered. My cancer was not straightforward, and I felt storm-tossed in a world of impossible trade-offs, with my life seeming to rest on the toss of coin.

In the coming months, with the care and support of family, friends and others, including unexpectedly from my work and business networks, I embarked on the third step, cycles of chemotherapy followed by cycles of a rare, proton beam, therapy. As treatment intensified in the run-up to the Christmas of 2024, so we left our home in Surrey and spent 5 weeks in Camden, North London, under the care of Oncology and Radiotherapy specialists at the Royal Marsden Hospital and University College London Hospital.

This project, the physical creation of my poetic anthology, was set aside, while always being a presence in the background. All my energy and attention, taken up by the consuming experience of those darker moments lived alongside moments of hope and joy, In the deep shadows of this third step into the world of cancer, I was left facing the comfort and desolation of answered and unanswered "Questions".

Until the moment I am at now, my fourth step. I've endured the treatment, lost weight, struggled with eating and taking on sufficient nutrition, and am now facing into a slow recovery, With relief, pleasure and surprise I find I have the energy to work on the anthology once again, and this time with a clearer intent. I feel encouraged once more to read the first line of the poem " My Questions":

"My Questions are my friends that grab me as I go..."

I am home now and can look out onto the rocks and patterns of my zen garden, pleased to be here with you at this "Starting Point". This is my provocation and invitation to us all, to step into a new conversation, a richer way of being together.

Let us begin!

Mirror

This chapter groups together illustrations and poems of moments when we see ourselves mirrored in situations we encounter.

You ask for what I look for?

I look for you.
And the sound of your step.
Will you walk with me?
So that we may keep enjoying
Seeking and looking together?

My Questions

My questions are friends
That grab me as I go
Like bristling thistles with spikey seeds
They wander; flutter then stick.

There are the ones I was
    born with
That share every passing
    joy
They remember all
    birthdays
And wipe every stinging or
    bitter tear.

Some I rarely see as they
    are kept
Hidden for when times get tough
Then gentle hedges they grow around me
Strong safe girds along tricky and treacherous paths.

Then some are stealthy creepers
This kind are only seen at night
Yet their sneak is not to haunt or taunt
It is simply to see if I am sad.

I know that a few cannot be friendly
As they are sworn never to stoop nor stay
On approach they search for my acknowledging eye
Then deftly they slip and gently slide away.

But my favourites are the silent ones
That somehow still find my ear
Caressing my lobe and whispering
Sweet truths as yet unheard.

My delight is that all come kindly
Cast in garbs curious and bright
Beckoning and signalling for attention
Lest distracted I might miss their spiriting flight.

TIRED EYES

I walk.
Along the way, I find myself.
A little worn, somewhat forlorn
Looking sorry, I think…
And very much alone.

I am torn,
Caught between care and
    pity
A rush of compassion?

I shudder…
Perhaps it's disdain.

Am I to blame,
I mutter - feeling breath
    hasten
As I turn askance
Only to see my own self's
Appeal gaze back plaintively at me
Through his silent
Tired eyes.

No, this cannot be the way
This should not be the path
I might have turned right
He could have looked left
Now, hastening past
I wonder at how we all happened
To turn out.

Complete

What do you look for? (You ask)

An ecstacy complete
Sustained and content
In need of nothing else
Other than itself
All embracing
Yet non referential
Truly deeply expressive
Constantly free
Not yearning or turning to
    see
What stands beyond
Nor behind or beneath:
As there is nothing to be
    found
And no one else to be freed.

What do you seek? (You beseech)

Being beyond any notion of travel
Yet knowing beginning from end
A destination alien
Yet felt as truly home
An arrival to a place
Unknown that wraps its familiarity around me.
Finding no need to walk
Yet enjoying every new and starting step.

What do you pursue? (You press)

Feeling every motion as making sense
And every sense filled with emotion
Vicariously happy
Never fearing fragility
As sadness and pain
Is the feeling of happiness passing
So still and breathing:
Not seeking or waiting
For this magical moment to wane.

Then where may you find rest at? (You entreat)

Walking alone but never feeling lonely.
Cheering with crowds
yet hearing each persons quietened chanter.
Finding the storyline
hidden within the poetry.
Telling the story through the beat of this poem.

You ask me what I long for?

A vibrant dynamic
Encompassing all and accepting eternity
Fulfilling and settling this
And every continuing longing.

You ask for what I look for?

I look for you.
And the sound of your step.
Will you walk with me?
So that we may keep enjoying
Seeking and looking together?

Dragons, Dens and Empty Spaces

Walking, talking and sleeping with Dragons
Stepping down
Letting go
Listening to the flutter

Finding space, sitting
Standing inside,
Looking...

Outside again
Seeing afresh
Still
Dragons...

Now with dens
And empty spaces
Smiling faces
Learning...

To breath (again)

What a joy...

Nails Chewed

Nails chewed and I wonder
Is this anxiety...
or comfort?
Could it be I could slip out
Now,
Well before the sticky end?

I hear the cynics' lament
"These things never end well"
I tremble...
I fear this piper's pay
Is in currencies
I no longer possess.

Will this stop?
So, I may step off
And if not
May I take my leave now
Before their shouting begins?

This heaviness
I carry
Lightly as an act
I thought
Yet now I am bowed beneath it
As scene turns
And play ends.

What speaks out now
Is truth provoked out of silence
Repeating in ancient tongue
What was lost in the modern translation.

So, we see what we know and fear
That what ends
Only ends when it does
And when we are gone
We'll still be here
Exit left or right
We are not sure you'll care.

So, sit up and look straight
Eyes soft and legs crossed
Then with quiet breath
Set wandering mind at rest
Knowing now as always before
How hard it is
To leave these nails.

This Story

This story has chosen
To seek me out.

It's hanging by
As if wanting a companion.

Its whisperings
Are in strangely familiar
Tongues,
Speaking to me
Or perhaps about me.

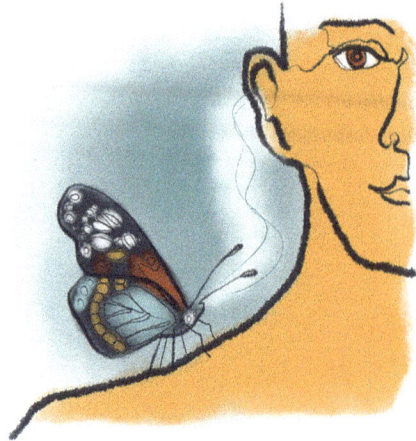

I feel it's timbre.
The sympathies of a kindred spirit
A friendly phantasmas
Breathing within me,
But novel
And not simply of my making.

Today this narrative
Is happy to be mine
Willing to be given
My fresh take
And with attentive touch
Happy to be making, with me
This new outing.

Flickering Flame

This life is flickering
quivering,
shimmering
Always fraught.

Clicketing
quickening,
fluttering,
Never caught.

Bold,
taut,
aflame.

Ever brighter.
Haute.

Arise!
This Dawn.

Fine and OK

I'm fine.
It's OK.
Even now as I feel this
    pain
Of needing to fight
When not knowing why
    or how
So, right now
I have to be OK
Not yet to be OK.

My Friend...
It's OK
Even now as I fight this fear
Of shining a faint light
When walking in a deepening dark
So, I guess now
It's got to be OK
Not yet to be OK.

My Love!
It's OK
Even now as I breath this sigh
Of releasing relief
When I see I'm here with you
So, I sense now
We're quite OK
Not yet to be OK

Stewardship

This chapter groups together Illustrations and poems around moments and experiences of collaboration and caring, when we are invited to take up the responsibilities that come with collaborating, caring for and looking after what sustains ourselves, our relationships and others.

HOPE WORE A GREY JUMPER

Bobbled and torn
Stretched at the neck
Nondescript, even dull...
Pointing and whispering
From deep within the Crowd.

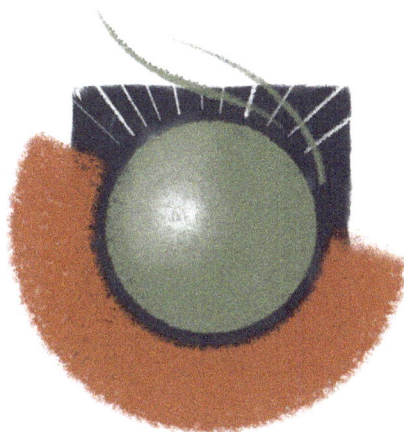

PAUSE

Pause.
Weave (back) into life
What brings (us) joy
Honouring lost honesty.

Brace.
Reach (in) once more
To halt (this) distress
To restore failing integrity.

Feel.
Seek (out) and grasp
This (last) passing hope
A wish wrapped in a prayer
Searching for a home.

Sit.
Quietly (still) and content
That this (present) moment
Will stay beyond this passing day
Holding firm and tight
So that all that is good
Is truly let loose.

LAST CALL

Scentless flowers
Tasteless buds
A bad itchy scratchy dream
That I can't wake up from.

Sleepless nights
Breathless days
Mouths propped open
Grasping for air.

No respite tonight
Forget redemption
Until tomorrow.

Hot days merge into
Windy nights
Fanning into fires
Our never-ending desires.

This emergency
Is a last call to all
Exercise your agency
For once, for all
And this once for good.

And yes,
For life!

SITTING WITH HER
ON THE HEATH

At the top of the hill
Once again seeking
Fleeting Serenity's illusive
    lair
Familiar failure beckons
Yet this time falters and
    gasps
Stumbling in awe
Yielding to bow
In the presence
Of Mother.

Acknowledging Her
I let free Her faint
Footsteps to fade
As I ignore the curving finger
Seeking my attention
For I too must now pause
And sit quite still
To witness Mother
Sharing Herself making
This moment go on
Forever.

I sense I am still summoned
Called here from my haste
Back to an innocence
Now only glimpsed
By those of spirit and courage
Free but good enough
To slip the shank
That binds calm within
Subject and tied to searching
And turmoil without.

So chastened I kneel to pray
That no one jumps in
Crassly without grace
Or moves out
Suddenly out of place
Unaware that in still silence
She more clearly and firmly
Speaks.

Because here
In the theatre of wonders
Our awakening breathes
New life into each sigh
Changing us back
Into our self-same selves
So that re enchanted
This moment of faith
Is forever protected and hidden
Not and never to die
In us.

Waiting To Be

There is something
Waiting to happen.

Not storming
nor stewing
Straining
or breaking.

Something forming.

Not brewing
nor cooking
Frowning
or fretting

Something shaping.

Not gasping
nor churning
Crying
or trying.

Just breathing.

Pregnant
Waiting.

Wanting to
Be.

August 2017

THESE THREE

Hope wore a grey jumper
Bobbled and torn
Stretched at the neck
Nondescript, even dull...
Pointing and whispering
From deep within the Crowd.

Faith heard his quiet gesturing
Setting her astir
Tugging at the heart
Persisting, even urgent...
Beckoning towards a Path.

Love was hard waking
Quietly seeking refuge
Sickened by cynical flirts
Wary, even fleeing...
Hiding from graceless starts.

But now,
Stirring to Hope's quiet gesturing
To trust this gathered mass.

Now,
Awakened by Faith's moving
To sooth fear-wearied eyes.

Now,
Rising, this threesome...
Again, for this worthwhile walk
...this ready crowd
Once stilled to "a sleep"
And now,
No more!

Still – Life

This chapter groups together Illustrations and poems of moments when we see life sitting still in front of us, inviting and / or provoking us to deepened insight.

TWO NOT YET LOVERS

Sitting
Hands touching
Solitary bluebells
Expectantly alone
In a soon to be crowded
Dell.

DISTURBED

The problem with poetry
He said,
Is that it disturbs your head.

But that wouldn't be just the poetry
Or simply your head,
She said.

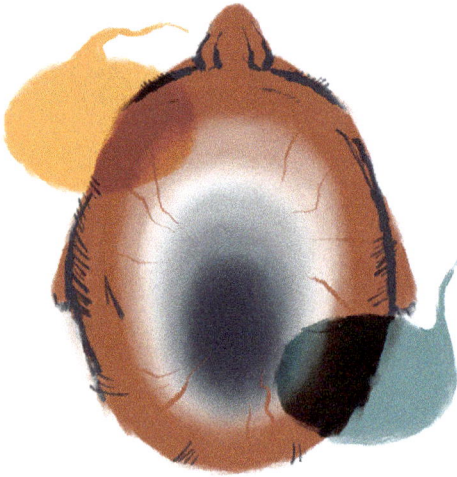

Bluebells

Two not yet lovers
Sitting
Hands touching
Solitary bluebells
Expectantly alone
In a soon to be crowded
Dell.

LOOK AT THIS MAN

Look at this man
So devious, so cruel
That he seeks from heaven
What he is taking from the crowd.

Feedback

It's a gift, she said.
For me... I asked?
For you... He replied.
From whom, I sighed...?
From your friends ...They cried!
Mmmm... I mused.
I didn't know I had any...
Not here.
Not now.
Not - At Work!

THE TRAM AT ST JOSEPH'S

The tram at St Joseph
Keeps on going...
Early in the morning
Before you and I Start
To late at night...
When you and I have
    Stopped.

I sit here and wonder
IF – I were in charge...
Where would I take it?
Where might I alight?

The tram at St Joseph
Has nothing to say...
Its joy is to trundle
Up this same hill...
Calling and crawling
Happily each day.

Calling

This chapter groups together Illustrations and poems of moments when we hear ourselves being summoned to attend to something deeper in us and the world, which we may have set aside or overlooked and now needs attention.

AND IF

After uninvited Challenge
And Effort, and Stretch, and all...
It all comes to nought - Except
That we stood
Gentle and honest
Loving and true.

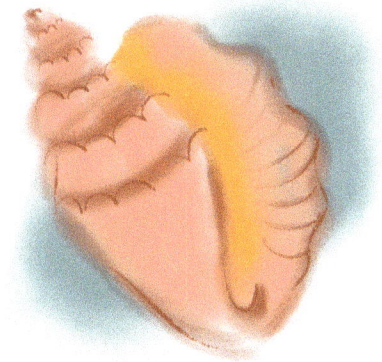

Not Yet Done

I am the story they haven't
    told
The song we shouldn't sing
The game you forgot to play.

I am the walk that's still to be
    had
The drink yet to be imbibed
The meal still to be cooked.

I am the man hiding in a boy
The woman silenced as a girl
The children now scattered and lost

In this fire pit I still smoke
A glowing ember
Not out yet
Still smouldering
Promising
A flame yet to blaze.

Yet still I may become
The rainbow after the storm
The handshake that stops the fight.

A hope, possibly
Even a heartfelt embrace
A burning honesty
Open enough at last
For this continuing truth.

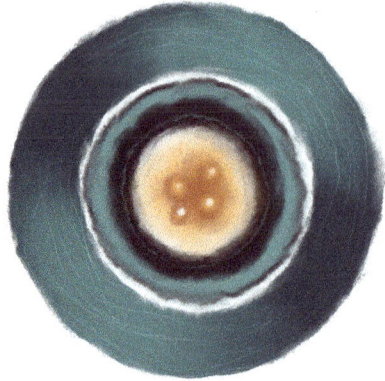

GLIMMER

In today's glimmer
Is the flight of an escaping
    heart
Fleeing an eclipsing past
Searching for a worthy soul
With whom to ponder
The musings of a wonderous
    universe.

In tonight's shimmer
Is the return of a hoping spirit
Seeking silently for a friend
To brave the depths of these blackest holes
A courageous venture of light
Into the dark night of an unknown galaxy.

Tomorrow's mummering
May herald the end of thankless yearnings
A time to pause...
Finally, to face that day
When we can release into doom
Frantic fretting and tiresome frowning.

So, in mysterious history
Remains our still steadfast faith
That in truths still hidden
Lie safe the birth secrets of life
Beauties concealed beyond ancient time
Enfolded in this moment
Pulsing, spirited, and precious
The life-giving gasp of a first breath.

LA PAIX

Is this not a way
To be with those that are
    unseen
So that they too can live
Not having to choose
Which strong man to
    please?

Is this not the place
Where we feel the strong
    grace of the lost
The unheard
Where we discover that
    doves too
Can fly free
Of olives and branches?

Was this not the hill
Where height signalled width
And breadth
Where commitment remained safely anchored
In our deepest sense of humanity?

Will this be the avenue
We can still walk on peacefully
And together
Where our hearts and your hopes
Will no longer lie separate
Hiding and afraid
Even though we share nests perched
Precariously in the same tree?

Is this not the life
We have shared and shaped these many years
That calls us to love and live on
Now.
Even as we descend this rise
And seek an avenue on a hill
Far less known
Yet never forgetting the path - that was La Paix
Where we were taught to be
And learned to become?

Break the Mould

Can you bring me
A hate that can be loved
A faith that could be shook
A hope that can be kept...
Can you?

Could you show me
The place I can stand
A space that I could share
A truth that *can* be kicked...
Could you?

Will you find me
A hand I can hold
A future I could mould
The gem I would hold...
Will you?

AND IF

And if
In vain indolence
This Princeling
Believes his ill-gotten Crown

And if
This Knave
Finds fleeting comfort
     snuggling
In a stolen robe

And if
After uninvited Challenge
And Effort, and Stretch, and all...
It all comes to nought - Except
That we stood
Gentle and honest
Loving and true

What frustrating gain
Is truly lost...
Anyway?

AT DAWN

At dusk
Puzzled and perplexed
Bewildered and hurt
Vexed...
Do Nought!

At dawn
Redeemed by rest
Freed from contempt
Blessed...
Be Brave!

WALK

Walk!
Barefoot.
Discover for yourself
The path
To life
To consolation.

Be!
Secure.
In redeeming love
Knowing
That through Grace alone
Who you are
Is more than
Enough.

Keep walking.
With courage and integrity
Making each step

An inquiring scrutiny
And a firm testimony.

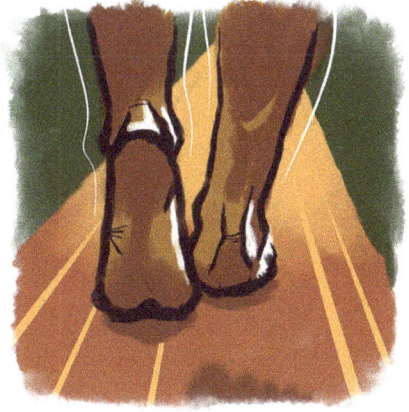

SHOW ME

Show me how to be present
To give myself
Silently to be there - and to be
    true.

Help me wholly to be my best
Listening....
Aware of my part right now...
Keeping prayers and dreams
    alive...
Discovering what is and what can be.

Strengthen me to find courage
in ordinary faces and places
Content to live and
Let life to be its own testimony.

Teach me again .... to play
To be like a child...
To laugh...
And care so deeply...
And have the nerve to show it.

Show me the small practical step,
To take...
... calmly, with faith
... with humility
Trusting and being thankful
for all that is provided.

THEN...

Then through power and with grace..
Let me wonder joyfully through life
Worshipful..
with friends and letters...
Wincing at history...
and..
Experiencing
More than it were fair for anyone
to experience...
In one short lifetime.

LE VAUD

Here in the cold
warming sunshine
the terrain may be steep
fog lurking and signalling
beckoning back
to lower horizons.

Yet higher light enchants
so, you stumble
and may even fall...
finding ground beautifully serene
yet in some place soft
even treacherous.

Curse!
Your foolish courage
and that again you are not
equipped...
that you are ill dressed -
Even now for this promising
endeavour.

Yet with each step
faith follows belief
finding once more
that for you
that are open and knowing.

You that are patient
hope-full and willing...

You that will walk
a little bit further
Up...
this stretching slope...

You who are
in good company
and with good enough sustenance...

For you...
Moments of discovery, wonder and new joy
Still...
await.

Mystery

This chapter groups together Illustrations and poems around when we are confronted with and invited to contemplate specific moments of mystery.

NOW I'M HERE

I am turned inside out...
Time does not mean anything
until Memory wanders uninvited
into view.

LOVE AND (THE LOGIC OF) POSSIBILITY

When mishaps and missteps lead
Sweet patterns can still shape
So that a sweet harmony of
    emotion
Forms strong and unbidden
Calling logic and reason to fall
Curiously into step.

Crystal clear stays misty
    mysterious
Notations still fail to tell
Whence I come from nor where
    I go
And why I pause
Now wide eyed, childlike, still aghast
Breath held in and caught
In wondering deepest awe
Even as this late evening sun
Promises a slower setting light.

Then, atop this tired being
A quietest cowrie in this head drops
A hollow tap, echoes in the old calabash
(Maybe this I can claim as the starting moment of wisdom)
A most important discovery
The eureka that makes this none-sense
And the day's scratching thirst
Now refreshed and quenchingly clear.

In these mysterious equations of life
Love is the only logical reason.

Repeating each time the same
Yet each time recurring never.

So, I may see I'm only here now
Because there is a reason that you are.

The possibility that separated musings
Can fall clear and drop silently into one another.

And our deepest reasons mysteriously
This day distil ever more deeply into each other.

Becoming true together:
Good and understood justifications
Standing proudly now enjoined in love
Entwined and bonded
Beyond solitude
And beyond logic.

After Midnight's Deeper Sleep

Now.
Closer to midnight
I fret.
Sensing that soon -
 this *search* must end
There will not again be the
 choice
This *quest* - must pass to
 another.

Even now.
Seeing that my *reckoning*
Having not happened
This *darkening* - must once
 again be left to be
Happily, un-done!

So now - *I*
May yet give *me* a way
Free to speed - to let
Tired grip slip mercifully, *silently*
Towards even deeper...
Deepening...
Sleep.

In Recovery

Not knowing how it would be afterwards
I didn't have anything planned
So being here today is different.

I am experiencing a future
In which I haven't any
        intention
I am arriving into a present
Without having any
        expectation.

The question is not how to
        slow down
And become aware
There is no question pressing
        forward right now...
None offering itself.

Until I form some kind of intent
Awareness is not in my head.

Sensations need a beckoning partner
to realise their shape.
Being here has nothing to do
With the thinking
In my head.

I am not alone
But they are not with me.
They are around me and
I'm trusting them.
They are there for me
But leaving me alone.

Right now
Their world is not mine...
Still they walk across my path
As it was a promise they made
Before this,
Long ago before we ever met.

And last week they said
(again) that they would...
It was because (rarely)
I had (and could make) a request.

Now as we meet here
They bring Questions...
Intention takes shape
And their Questions jump -
Towards me.

They first tickle my innards
Before creeping through my belly
Reaching for pathways to my head.

Then I have to speak:
To express The Intention
One that may reluctantly
Re-connect me
With their world,
Ushering forward.

New now-intending self
The one my "helpers" have decided
To shape me into
in this conversation today.

If I dodge them
I can stay here
As I have not been here before
Not all of me...
I've wondered past
but never found this door.

Now I'm here
I am turned inside out...
Time does not mean anything
until Memory wanders uninvited
into view.

I'm not rushing by
As time will stop for useless distraction
(She is dressed differently today)
I can see her and her mates clearly though
I'm old enough to see them now.

I do not want to go...
If I get up, I must show intent...
Helpers will see me.
I think I may let them.
They are many
But at least I know
Some maybe serving friends.

I fear though that I might
then have the urge to hold them.
Too soon to seek
to answer
to tame and to own.

Schedules may arise
I may re-join
The race.

I haven't been here before
and somehow
it feels like I've found a home.
One that I am loath ever to leave.

GONE

I dream that I may...
Walk out to Appear..
Elsewhere...
Maybe touch the World...
Without meaning.... to touch,
It...
In a different way...

Like traveling ...
Walking a new road...
With each step meaning something...
Else...
Laden with a significance
Strangely felt...
But not in my first creation meant...
Only now in present conception fully grasped...

Then somewhere!
Yet a murmuring...
A quivering strength that didn't exist...
A being...
A will...
Owing me no attention...
Yet felt kin-ly resonant..

So yet may I be content
Again to walk on...
Untouching
Touching
Untouched
Touched
Gone.

END NOTE

We live life in fast prose punctuated by insistent poetic moments. Stories we tell are animated and intensified by metaphor and image. The rhythm and cadence of what we observe, say, and feel takes us into the deep impact of experiences we carry in our hearts, which imprint themselves in our minds and bodies. Poetic portals litter our lives with morsels of meaning and insight. We can choose to follow, feed or ignore them. If we miss them - harried by our rushing through each moment, our eyes set on the next thing, the goals we have, the never-ending plans and commitments we are carrying, these moments stay quietly with us, biding their time. Until something we see, say or feel stirs them and calls them back into sight.

Our attention captured; the poetic moments beckon us to conversations that have been waiting for us, some easy, some not. We need the poetic moments to guide us, be our trusted invitations into deepened experience and understanding – an aid to settle our frenetic minds, and so find we can become open to a world of new, and different perspectives.

This is my collection of poetic moments. Offered as invitations to conversations. Each relates to an event, observation, thought, or experience, that has disrupted my harried forward focused too-ing and froing - stopping me in my tracks, making me notice, and leaving me disturbed, unsettled and awakened. In time the discomfort settles, and when rested, calmed or simply made safe through distance and time passing, the poetic moments turn into these fuller expressions.

Feelings, scents and images become words. Inquiry no longer a threat but now an inspiration. New perspective ushers in different insights and energies. Emotions step out of their cage. Heroic words flow - sometimes few, at times many - expressing this disturbing and unsettling experience in a heartfelt and understood poetic moment. This is the starting point for a deeper conversation you are invited into, about what you now see, notice, love, feel, dislike, reject, appreciate, seek, acknowledge and find yourself willing to **be inspired by**.

Acknowledgements

These acknowledgments can only start in one place. With my family. They have accompanied me as I have gathered these poetic scribblings and continue to walk with me now.

My dear wife Tanya, who I fondly refer to as my "secret weapon" has been and remains my inspiration and tower of strength and support.

My daughters Alex and Robyn, whose gentle almost daily encouragements have helped me through some of the darker more difficult moments of recovery.

Alistair and Gabriel, stalwart and strong, I appreciate you dearly guys.

Finlay and Ellis, our grandsons, your encouragement to me through this time is greater than you will ever know.

Beyond that others who have been part of the making of this unfolding story: Jade Jeries, Lindsay Wittenberg, John Higgins and Anne-Marie Miller. Without your support and contributions, this would be a much lesser piece of work.

And finally, my faithful friends and some particularly supportive clients, (you know who you are!) through the extended period of treatment and personal challenge, you have stayed in touch encouragingly. Some of you also provided practical financial assistance that has made it possible for me to complete this piece of work. I thank you all!

Anthony Kasozi
Ashtead, Surrey – March 2025

About the Author

"Starting Points" is a selectively curated anthology of poems written by Anthony Kasozi and offered as an "invitation to conversation"

The book presents 31 poems grouped in 5 chapters "Mirror"; "Stewardship"; "Still Life" "Calling" and "Mystery" reflecting the different types of provocations and invitations that evoked them.

As poetry most comes alive when it is heard rather than simply read, readings of these poems can be found on the author's website: www.anthony-kasozi.info/poetry.

Anthony is a tutor-writer and coach mentor – founder director of Quilibra, a consulting and resource facility supporting leaders and teams working to address challenging developmental and change issues and contexts.

www.ingramcontent.com/pod-product-compliance
Lightning Source LLC
LaVergne TN
LVHW010305070426
835508LV00026B/3438